Improve Your Virtual Meetings

By John Arthur

Contents

Introduction

The world is moving toward doing more remote work, which means more virtual meetings.

At the same time, your personal brand is more important than ever. Everything you do in a professional setting – and how you do it – reflects on the reputation you are creating for yourself. If how you show up in a virtual meeting makes a weak impression, the effects reverberate through all aspects of your career.

It wasn't that long ago when a meeting meant just one thing: Gathering in an office or conference room, and in some cases getting in a car or on an airplane to do it, to sit across the table or next to others, and have a discussion. Those times are gone.

Today, doing business or having discussions over phone calls, conference calls, or, increasingly, video calls is becoming more and more common.

We have been getting to this new normal for many years, but it really accelerated in the past decade. The advent of the virtual meeting began with the person-to-person phone call, and stayed that way for many years. The choices were to either meet in person, or to do a phone call.

Then, multi-person calls became more common. They were originally done by merging multiple phone calls together to create a multi-party call. They were good if you only needed three people on the line, but they were clunky.

The next step of evolution was the conference bridge -- a gamechanger. The conference call is a thing of both incredible value but also some disdain and ridicule. Conference calls opened up our world to easy-to-access multi-person meetings, meetings that could have 2 people or 1,000 people. The conference call culture and norms are still evolving, but today conference calls make up a sizeable chunk of all meetings, and have established their place in organizational and corporate culture alike.

The next wave of evolution, and one that I think has yet to crest, is the videoconference. While such video meeting types have been around for 10-20 years, it is only relatively recently that they moved from novelty to must-have status for many organizations.

I don't see the trend of taking our meetings and interactions virtual declining anytime soon. In fact, with new collaboration tools constantly being created by our entrepreneurial class, I think adapting to new modes of collaboration and virtual interactions will become more important with every passing year. If you are just starting out in your career, making these channels second nature will pay off. If you are deep into your career, adapting to these communication forms will allow you to make your maximum contribution.

When I wrote my first book, I devoted several of the chapters to the importance that communication can have on your career. Becoming effective in settings like conference calls and video conferences is more than a nice-to-have. It is increasingly an imperative if you want to perform and advance in certain organizations. It is important if you want your organization to function in a decentralized environment. And it is critical if you want your response to events like travel stoppages (whether they are due to public health or budgetary reasons) to be one that does not disrupt business-as-usual.

"Start with the Why."

—Simon Sinek, Author

The Importance of Building a Virtual Meeting Skill

The number of video and audio meetings increases, seemingly, by-the-week.

Video and audio conferences are having a bigger role in our society than they were just a couple years ago, and this is probably a good thing. There are many reasons for this increased importance. Indeed, as society becomes more and more reliant on technology, the same can be said for conferences and how we collaborate.

In the past, audio and video conferences were not really possible. Technology was not powerful enough to allow for large scale discussions and conferences to be held, and when they were held they were typically expensive and clunky. This limited the number of people that could be reached with and participate in video and audio conferencing technology. Recent advancements and the rapid development of technology, connectivity networks, and the like mean virtual meetings are the default communication option in many situations.

Nowadays, technology is able to accommodate hundreds or potentially thousands of conference goers at once. This offers a huge number of benefits for conferencing and so, the importance of video and audio conferencing is undeniably growing at a rapid rate. And this opens up a number of possibilities for the future of conferencing, too, that would simply have been impossible with the limited possibilities offered by conferences held in person with a physical audience.

Technology Bandwidth has Opened New Doors for Us

One of the major limitations of video and audio conferencing in the past was that of technology bandwidth allowances. Indeed, sharing conference calls with multiple people from around the world would once have been an impossibility.

In the early days of the internet, of course, it was obvious why this would not be possible. You might remember it -- downloading an image took 20 seconds. The sheer power required to livestream a conference call would have simply been unimaginable. However, even in recent years, audio and video conferencing has not been an easy goal to achieve.

Not that video and audio are the same in this regard. A standard video call, compared to video conferencing, has far lesser demands on bandwidth. Assuming that high quality video is important—which, of course, is essential for any important call—every participant would put up the bandwidth requirements by about 1 Mbps per second, and 1.5 Mbps is preferred.

According to Skype, the provider of conference services, a video call takes about 15 times as much bandwidth as an audio call, and video calls with multiple people demand more bandwidth in proportion to the number of attendees.

To put that bandwidth in perspective, most homeowners in developed countries nowadays will have an internet connection of about 30 Mbps, on average (according to Cable.co.uk, from data gathered in 2019). Furthermore, the average global bandwidth was just over 11 Mbps in 2019. As such, it is easy to see just how much power would be needed for a conference call with many, many viewers.

Given that the average bandwidth per office or household has increased at an impressive clip over the past 20 years, it is easy to see why virtual meetings are so much more possible today than they were a few years ago.

Freelancers and Digital Nomads are a Larger Part of the Economy

One of the key reasons that video and audio conference calls are becoming more popular is because more and more people are taking up freelance work. With freelance workers and digital nomads (people who use the internet for their main source of income and work) on the rise, the importance of audio and video conferencing has also increased sharply.

It is hard to come into the office for a meeting, when your office is your bedroom in a mountain town, 2,000 miles away.

This fact represents a significant challenge for traditional forms of conferencing. Because freelance workers and digital nomads typically work from home, many workers live hundreds or thousands of miles away from a business' main office—they might even live abroad, or be working while traveling abroad. Regardless of the reason, freelance workers and digital nomads will rarely need to attend a meeting in the office. And, as such, digital conferencing represents a great opportunity.

Virtual meetings are an important aspect of working with freelancers and digital nomads. These individuals do not need to spend excessive amounts of time traveling to an office that might be located many hours from their normal workspace. Instead, they can simply connect with a video or audio conference call from the comfort of their own home.

This is a useful development for so many reasons. As well as saving the workers time and money—which could be better spent elsewhere—it also allows a business to have a practical means of communication with these workers. Conferences and meetings can be arranged between freelance workers, living in different time zones, and this allows for effective team communications.

It also allows organizations to find and use the best talent available, regardless of where that talent lives.

In addition to saving money and providing for convenience, conference calls can also be arranged with very little notice being needed. In a modern world that is incredibly rapid, this is essential for allowing your team to respond to new developments in a rapid and timely manner. This can be hugely beneficial for freelance workers, who can also continue working right up until the point that the conference call begins.

A Worldwide Pandemic Accelerated Adoption

Virtual meetings were gaining in popularity and usage well before the COVID-19 pandemic, but there is no denying that the adoption of remote work was profoundly accelerated by the pandemic.

Before the spread of Coronavirus, platforms like Zoom, Teams, and Webex were growing at a steady pace, but nothing like they did in early 2020. Zoom usage exploded from 10 million users in December, 2019 to 100 million users just four months later. That kind of impetus for growth is the "Black Swan" event that can change how we work, and there are many indications that the modern workplace may never fully return to its pre-COVID state.

The percentage of American workers who were working from home during the pandemic mushroomed to 50%, from roughly 10% just a few months earlier. Business tripsStudies are showing that many of the employees and employers alike intend to not fully return to the office, but what that specifically means has yet to unfold.

I think it is safe to say that the pandemic permanently changed how we work, and how we communicate with each other, and that will make your ability to communicate in virtual environments only more important with each passing year.

The way to gain a good reputation is to endeavor what you desire to appear.

—Socrates

Working from Home Has Benefits: Retention, Expense Savings, and More

As already explained, freelance workers and digital nomads often spend a lot of time working from home. There are plenty of reasons as to why this style of working has become more popular! Indeed, the benefits of working from home mean that more and more people are choosing to become freelance workers, where possible—and this can have benefits for both businesses and their freelance workers, as well.

Staff Retention Rates

For a business, a key benefit of hiring freelance staff who work from home is in regards to the superior staff retention. This is largely due to the morale boost that can come from working at home. Forbes wrote that more than 80% of workers would like to be able to work from home, and other studies suggest that work-at-home programs reduce attrition by 50%.

Freelance workers often report being more comfortable when working from the comfort of their own home. In part, this is often due to the happy working environment; for many, not having to be a part of the chaos that is the modern office can be relaxing and highly enjoyable. Moreover, workers who work from home often enjoy not having to commute to work, allowing them more time to get ready for their working day without the stress of needing to arrive at the office on time. For workers who have flexible work times, this is further heightened.

All of these benefits can be very important for improving staff morale. And this, in turn, can be directly related to staff retention rates. Hiring new staff can be incredibly expensive for a business, and new staff members may also need additional training and may not be as efficient (and profitable) as more experienced staff members. As such, the importance of staff retention is clear, and creating a good working environment is important in this goal.

Expense Savings

The expense savings associated with allowing people to work from home really fall into two separate buckets: The expense savings you realize from allowing your employees to work in a decentralized way, and the ability to access freelance talent that might be less-expensive than making permanent, local hires.

For the worker, expenses go down too. After an initial cash outlay to properly outfit a virtual office (see my section on Equipment later in this book), the reduced cost of commuting, transit, parking, attire, restaurant meals, and even child care can really add up.

Back to the organizational perspective, perhaps the biggest savings is realized on the ability to access remote talent, and freelancers, on a job-by-job basis.

Being able to access staff from all corners of the world means that you can find great talent for much more competitive pay. Depending on the nature of your business, it is possible that your entire workforce could even be work from home workers; if this is the case, you won't really need a very big dedicated office for your business. This can offer substantial savings in terms of upfront purchasing costs or office rental costs.

It is not just the business that benefits, though. If you are a freelancer, the ability to open your base of potential clients to anyone in the world is a major benefit. Not to mention, you can live in a low-cost area and basically arbitrage the living expenses and wages of two very different geographies.

Direct employment costs are another major savings that organizations will see when moving workers home, whether they are employed or freelance. Office space rent costs anywhere from $1 per square foot in a smaller town to $80 per square foot in a place like San Francisco. On site workers then need to be provided with their own equipment, including all relevant technology. Furthermore, the equipment that they use will need to be powered; this means you will need to consider electricity bills and ongoing maintenance bills for the office. Finally, insurance and other regulatory mandates might increase the cost of on site employment even more, depending on the local laws and market.

There is also the additional consideration of worker profitability to consider, too. When you hire a virtual worker, you will likely find that they are more efficient due to increased worker morale and the ability to work the hours that best suit them, rather than forcing everyone into a 9-to-5 routine. This, in turn, will likely mean that your workers will give a better return on investment than if they were working in the office each day -- and there is a good chance you are paying them less on top of it. Furthermore, evidence is emerging that workers who work from home generally take fewer sick days and vacation time off work too which can also help to limit costs. This could be due to the ability to work in a solo environment while sick, less stress, more loyalty, or a combination of all three.

Access to More Talent

When you hire office workers, you are largely limited to those people who live locally to you. This can really limit the amount of talent that you can hire. However, when you choose to hire a work-at-home worker, you can suddenly get access to the highest skilled workers from all around the world! This will allow you to hire the best talent for your business, and this in turn will help you to make the most of the workers available to you and your business.

When your pool of possible staff is not limited to the people in your direct geographic area, it could make the difference between finding the perfect fit for your job, or settling for someone who is good enough. Most businesses will say that their people are what make them great, and being open to virtual work allows you to access the best staff.

Recent Viruses Have Shined a Light on Social Distancing

It has been a long time since the world has seen anything like the current COVID-19 outbreak. For all the damage it created, one silver lining is that I think that it started a trend of making home-work arrangements that probably will never fully reverse.

Social distancing is something that is incredibly hard in our modern world. Our society has been built with the ideals of cooperation in mind and the same can be said about our working environments, too. Our workplaces are built to fit as many people in as possible, on the whole; this, of course, means that we are ill equipped to deal with an outbreak such as we have seen in current times. The trend in recent generations has to become more urban and more community-focused.

The COVID-19 pandemic serves to highlight the importance of having measures in place to enable social distancing. Diseases such as Coronavirus spread rapidly due to close contact with other people who are suffering from the condition (even if they are not yet aware that they are ill).

Rapidly-spreading viruses can have a plethora of different impacts on businesses. People who are self isolating can mean a huge reduction in the size of the business' workforce, and an ill worker can rapidly spread the disease among their colleagues, thereby putting a large amount of the team out of work. This will impact on the business' income, productivity, and profitability. In fact, a lot of businesses are struggling due to the severe limitations being imposed upon them, with small businesses in particular at an especially large risk of being made bankrupt as a result of the disease.

However, there is a solution that businesses employ when an outbreak is occuring or imminent. By implementing audio and video conferencing technology, the business will be able to send its workers home and communicate with them directly. This is also relevant for workers who are voluntarily self isolating, as these workers can still be kept in the loop with business management. If the technology is in place, audio and video conferencing may even allow the business to operate at almost peak capacity, even if all of its workers are having to work from home and away from the office environment.

"Culture eats strategy for breakfast."

—Peter Drucker, Author

Advice to Organizations: It All Starts With Culture

While the target reader for this book is the worker or manager who wants to master their virtual meeting effectiveness, or the free agent or digital nomad, I feel it is important to say a few words to organizational leaders who may be reading it.

As with so many organizational efforts, becoming effective at virtual meetings all comes down to the culture of the organization. The organizational norms and expectations will determine if virtual meetings work, and if things like video conferencing truly get the traction that they can.

Defining when virtual meetings are the right tool, rules of engagement during the meetings, and the organization's overall commitment to virtual work are critical to aligning the team.

Define When Virtual Meetings are the Right Tool

The answer on if a virtual meeting is the right communication channel is different for every organization, and for every situation within the organization. I am close to some fast-and-nimble organizations who have the motto that virtual meetings are always the first choice, and they only want to get together in-person if absolutely necessary. I work with other organizations who are the opposite -- they say face-to-face is always best, and the virtual meeting is only done if a physical meeting just isn't possible.

Most organizations fall somewhere in between. They have a regular cadence of virtual meetings which allows people to avoid commutes, be more efficient with their time, and have quick "stand-up" meetings from wherever they are. Then, they reserve the more critical forums, especially the ones that require open discussion and idea generation, for times when they can be together in-person.

Have Crystal-Clear Rules of Engagement for Virtual Meetings

Setting a tone throughout the organization regarding how people are to engage in video or conference calls is critical. If people view virtual meetings as optional, your culture will never make the most of what could otherwise be effective communication channels.

Answer a few key questions within your organization, and then communicate them clearly and hold to the standard. Questions might include:

- Are your virtual meetings going to be via video, or audio conference?

- If virtual, are audio-only attendees acceptable or not?

- Where are people expected to be during such discussions? Is background noise acceptable?

- How do you define who has the floor?

- Who is responsible for the agenda and notes?

- Do you do a roll call so you know who is on the line? (I recommend you always do even if it seems silly)

- If somebody can't make it, should they provide advance notice? (Again, I recommend yes, otherwise calls might suddenly have partial attendance)

In short, it is all about clarity, shared understanding, and removing optionality. If you can achieve those things, your virtual meeting culture will begin to improve.

Demonstrate the Organization's Commitment to Virtual Work

To the leaders reading this, especially those responsible for setting the company tone and controlling the checking account, you can do small things to make an outsized impact on the traction that your virtual work and virtual meeting efforts get.

How can you enable the productive use of video and audio conferences and other virtual meetings?

First, signal that it is acceptable -- or even preferred -- to do business virtually rather than in-person. My first point in this chapter about defining which situations are appropriate for virtual meetings is a start. Then, follow-through and encourage it. Show that people can be productive regardless of where they happen to be working, and that you can actually *increase* your communication because you can talk more often and more easily. Lead by example, by being a fully-engaged and energetic participant in your organization's conference calls or video meetings. When you see a group that just traveled to have a 30-minute meeting on routine topics, suggest that they explore a virtual meeting.

Second, enable virtual and remote meetings by giving people the resources they need. If you are asking people to work from home, but you don't provide them with cell service, for example, you are at the whim of the plan that fits their family budget or perhaps them trying to do calls via computer wi-fi (more on that later). Quality will be compromised. Likewise, don't skimp on your video or audio conference service. Bad ones cause latency in calls, dropped conferences, and phone jams as people are attempting to dial-in. There is no bigger killer of the virtual meeting movement than a platform that doesn't work for your people.

Obey the principles without being bound by them.

—Bruce Lee

Key Principles to Remember About Working Virtually

Before I get into the details of conducting or participating in good video or audio conference, a note on virtual meetings. After all, having good virtual work habits, and good virtual meeting performances, go hand in hand.

When it comes to working virtually, there are many benefits. However, the change can be quite the shock for someone who has not worked from home before, and so being aware of some of the most important principles for working from home is important. This will allow you, or your business' workers, to make the most of the chance to work from home instead of working in a normal business office.

The Goal is to be More Productive

View working remotely -- whether it is working from home or working from your dream vacation spot -- as an opportunity to contribute more, and be more productive.

If you can find ways for your remote work to better blend your personal life, hobbies, family, and professional focus, you win. That is the goal.

In my book, _Manage Your New Career_, I advise people that the journey is the reward. Don't worry so much about the endgame, but rather enjoy the rewarding process of trying to get there. If working remotely can help you do that, then it is all worth it.

At the same time, your employer, or your customers (if you are self-employed) need you to be as productive as possible. If you can prove that you are fully-productive from a remote location, then it becomes a resounding win-win.

Have Dedicated Space for Working

One of the biggest difficulties associated with working from home is often finding the motivation to work. This is a big problem when there are so many distractions around. Working from home can often be great for morale, which can increase productivity, however the lack of routine and regulation can mean that staying focused can sometimes be a little difficult.

The key to this is to make sure that you have a dedicated space for working. Having a dedicated workspace is important as this will allow you to "get in the zone" and develop the right mindset for a productive work day.

Your dedicated workspace should ideally be one which is shielded from distractions – both for you, and the people on the other end of your virtual meeting. It should also be a comfortable place to work in, too; as such, your dedicated workspace should be one which has the adequate equipment for you to be able to work in comfort. If this means swivel chairs and wrist supports, get them—the difference that these little comforts will make for your ability to provide quality work will likely surprise you!

If you are not comfortable, you will likely struggle to work well. This is one of the biggest challenges that workers who have just started working from home will face. However, once you have a dedicated workspace established and set up, you will likely find that things are far easier and working from home will be a great experience.

Working from a Coffee Shop Is Not the Answer!

A common mistake that people make when trying to come up with a dedicated workspace is to choose a coffee shop or another loud place to work from. However, this absolutely should not be your primary workspace.

I get it. A coffee shop has nice background noise, a little visual interest, and caffeine. I have worked in coffee shops, too, but typically for an hour or so just for a change of scenery. Then, I am back in my home office, because I love working in it.

But if you are taking lots of meetings, whether audio or video, be cognizant of the impression your coffee shop works gives to the person on the other end of the meeting.

When working from home, distractions can be a major concern. Coffee shops are, by their very nature, filled with these distractions! The rich smells will likely serve to distract you from your work and make you want to have a snack, instead. In fact, the entire layout of the coffee shop will be tailored to this end; after all, the coffee shop exists to make a sale to you, and the marketing team will have done everything in their power to entice you to buy more.

Perhaps the major reason to not park yourself in a restaurant or coffee shop is the noise. If you take any phone calls at all, the sound of an espresso machine and the murmur or families around you is a major distraction to the person on the other end. Avoid it altogether if you can.

Call me old school, but working from home means working from **home** (or a suitable dwelling.) Work from public or subpar areas at your own peril.

Don't Skimp on Your Connectivity

When it comes to working from home, your internet connectivity might be the most important investment you make. It is key that you have a good internet connection. As discussed previously, a critical problem associated with audio and video conferencing is that of bandwidth and internet connectivity. As such, it is important that you make sure your internet connection is adequate before starting to work from home.

It is even more important if you plan to do video meetings, as they take up 15x the bandwidth that an audio call does.

In general, most high quality video connections require a bandwidth of approximately 1 Mbps; this will vary based on the quality of the stream and the number of people joining the video conference. If your bandwidth does not meet these requirements, you may want to consider upgrading your current internet connection or otherwise arranging for audio conferences instead of video conferences.

Dogs and Children: People Don't Want to Hear Them

When it comes to working from home, it is still important to maintain good professional standards. As part of this, it is important that you don't make video or audio conference calls when other loud noises might be around. Children and dogs are common nuisances for people trying to attend or otherwise make a video or audio conference, so make sure to arrange a time and a place for the conference where you can be away from these distractions.

Listen, I know that your children (if you have any) mean the world to you. Mine sure do to me. And having what I call a "human moment" here and there is probably OK. While having a child's voice or a dog's bark on the conference call can add some levity, it is best to avoid it altogether. You probably will never get to 100%, but try to get as close to that as you are able.

Stick to Routines

Working from home can sometimes be a bit difficult, often due to a lack of motivation. In order to combat this, it is imperative that you try to create routines for your daily working life. Creating routines, just like you would have in the workplace, will help you to ensure that you stick to your goals and your deadlines.

One of the great things about working from home, though, is that you can afford to occasionally adjust these routines if you need to; it is just important that you try to stick to routine for the vast majority of the time, as it can be incredibly easy to make excuses if you routinely begin to sway from your standard routine. But remember, you don't need to work tirelessly throughout the day! Make sure that you include regular breaks and chances to get up and stretch during your working day.

I even know some successful professionals who get semi-dressed up for work even if they are just doing email and audio conferences all day. The fact that they are in dressier attire triggers better habits that result in better productivity.

One of the tricks to being productive at home is to have a regular "starting time".

Starting work at the same time every day is a good way to make sure that you still have routine in your life, even when working from home. Furthermore, starting work early is also a great way to shake off the sluggishness of sleep that may have otherwise been holding you back. Studies have found that most workers find themselves feeling more motivated during the early hours, so if this is also the case for you, make sure to set aside time in the morning for doing your work.

Not everyone is overly bright and chirpy in the early hours, though. If you happen to be one of the lucky "night owls" who work better in the later hours of the day, though, don't worry about forcing yourself to work in the morning unless your schedule dictates it; if you have freedom to choose when you work, then by all means do most of your work in the evening. Just be on a schedule somewhat similar to the rest of the world.

Make Time for Video and Audio Conferences

Working at home requires strict self control, however, it can also be incredibly satisfying and fulfilling. The freedom that the work from home lifestyle can offer makes it an attractive working arrangement for many. As such, it is clear that more and more people are beginning to try working from home themselves.

However, if you or your employees are working from home, it is still important to have contact. Video and audio conferencing represents an excellent means of communication for businesses and their workers who are working from home. Direct conferencing allows team meetings to be held remotely and clear instructions can be given, which may be hard to explain through messages. This will only work, though, if both parties can find a suitable time to have these audio or video conferences; so, if you or your team are working from home, make sure that you arrange a suitable time to have these conference calls, if they might be needed on a regular basis.

One final trick -- always block the 15 minutes prior to a big, important video call, and ideally at least 10 minutes prior to an audio conference call, to prepare. Test the equipment, make sure you know what the topic is, and read any pre-reads. If everyone does that, you will avoid those awkward first few minutes when everyone is trying to get their technology working and figuring out what the meeting is about.

All the sounds of the earth are like music.

—Oscar Hammerstein

How to be a Pro at Conference Calls

First, I will talk about conference (non-video) calls, as a conference call requires some techniques that are unique and not always shared with video meetings, which I will discuss in the next chapter.

As I mentioned in the last chapter, becoming good at audio conference calls takes some practice, and some intentionality. Here are some tips and techniques gleaned from years of coaching employees, reading the available literature, and being on calls myself.

If hosting or participating in an audio conference call is not normal for you, it can seem a little difficult or awkward to start with. Luckily, once you start conferencing, you will likely pick up on the skills that you need to be able to fully participate and provide excellent communications using the channel.

If you have done hundreds of audio conference calls but just want to be more effective on them, some of these tips will be equally useful for you.

It All Starts With the Right Space

You would be amazed at how sensitive today's audio technology can be, and how much background noise can be picked-up by a call! If 6 people are on a conference call, and 1 is in a noisy place and the other 5 are in a quiet place, the 1 noisy one sticks out like a sore thumb.

Even background noise, like noise from a nearby busy road, could interfere with your connection and make it hard for people to hear you or the speaker. At a minimum, it creates a distraction. As such, plan ahead and find somewhere that is as silent as possible. The ideal place for a conference call is a room which is closed in and blocked off from outside noises. It doesn't need to be large or pretty. Furthermore, you also need to make sure that anyone (or anything) nearby that could cause a disturbance is unable to get into your conference space.

Try not to be that person who disrupts the conference call because their toddler came in asking for something loudly, or because the dog started barking for dinner in the background. I get it, it happens, but don't let it happen with regularity. Make the right preparations in advance to make sure that your conference space is quiet, calm, and free from disturbances.

Invest in Quality Audio Gear

Audio technology is exceptional nowadays. However, not all audio gear is made the same! It pays to invest some money in the equipment for audio calls, especially if you plan to make them a regular part of your culture. Choosing equipment for your, or your team's, conference call setup.

I decided to write a standalone chapter on the topic of virtual meeting technology, so you could easily reference it whenever you need.

Again, I provide more information in my chapter on virtual meeting equipment.

Consider Augmenting your Computer Microphone

The microphones on new computers have improved dramatically over where they were even a year or two ago. You can now trust that your computer or laptop microphone will get the basic job done, if your intent is to relay information or participate in general meetings.

However, the voice quality when speaking into a computer is usually underwhelming, especially if there is any background noise whatsoever.

Especially on aged computers, the voice quality when you speak over a laptop or desktop is grainy, thin, and often interrupted. The speaker quality of the audio coming back at you is equally bad if not worse.

An external microphone – the kind that podcasters use to record their shows – can really make a difference in your voice sound quality. If you are someone who is leading a large group of people, involved in important sales meetings, or doing other PR-type work where delivering the message is critical, consider investing in an external microphone.

One external mic I like right now is the Tula microphone. It is portable, has great sound quality, cancels unwanted noise well, and is small enough so it stays out of sight if you don't want it to be prominent during your meetings. I put it just off to the side of my computer during my Zoom meetings, and it works great. You can find it here on Amazon.

Have An Agenda

Some of the advice for virtual meetings is really regular meeting advice, except certain points are made even more important because of the situation. Having an agenda falls into that category.

A big part of any successful conference call is for everyone to understand why they are even there, and what you are trying to accomplish. The agenda will help you to make sure that all of the most important points are covered during the conference call, which can often be hard to achieve without an agenda that everyone can see. An agenda is also important for keeping the meeting on time. Conference calls run the risk of being notoriously-poorly managed, especially if half of the attendees are trying to multitask.

But how can you make an agenda? Making an agenda doesn't need to be difficult, but it is important that you follow a few set rules to check your agenda will cover everything that is needed in the conference and keep things running smoothly.

Tips for Creating the Perfect Conference Agenda

Without an agenda for your conference, you will likely find yourself struggling to meet deadlines and cover all of the points for your conference. As such, the importance of creating an agenda in advance cannot be overstated. Your event agenda will make sure that all of the topics required of the conference can be covered. Furthermore, a well formed agenda is also essential for time management at the event.

A good agenda is the backbone of a successful conference. The agenda is important for both the organisers of the conference call, as well as for listeners of the event. The agenda will help the organisers of the conference call to monitor statistics of the conference call and analyze areas of interest and areas of lesser engagement with listeners.

When creating an agenda for your conference call, you will first want to think about the outcomes you are looking for. What are factors that need to be discussed? Is the purpose of the meeting to provide status or take action? Is it a single-topic meeting (I recommend those) or a broad agenda?. This will ensure that the conference call goes smoothly and covers all of the points that need to be raised, and does so in the time allocated. Furthermore, it will allow all of the listeners of the conference call to have their own queries and concerns raised, thereby creating an engaging conferencing opportunity for all listeners involved.

A good agenda needs to be well laid out and organized. Once you have decided on the topics that you wish to discuss during the audio conference, you should then assign a set period of time to each of these areas of discussion. A conference call can easily go on for too long, so assigning a slot for each topic will help you manage the time well. This will prevent the conference from dragging on for too long, and will make sure that every point of discussion remains engaging for the listeners of the audio conference.

If you have important points, put them at the top of the agenda so they do not get bumped. If you will be asking others to speak on specific content, give them a heads-up so they are prepared.

Creating an agenda doesn't need to be hard. Make sure to get input from all of the listeners of the event. This will allow the event to go without a hitch, ensuring attendee engagement and a successful conference call.

If you are not leading the meeting, but participating, review the agenda in advance, and jot down any points that you want to make. This will help you contribute more productively.

Think Carefully About Timing

This point has to do with both the time allocation within a meeting, but also the overall time of the meeting and its placement on a calendar. When creating your conference call's agenda, it is important to allocate time carefully (and then stick to this during the audio conference itself). If a topic is urgently important to discuss, put it at the beginning of an agenda. If you want to encourage discussion on a particular subject, do not allocate 5 minutes to it… give it room to run.

Beyond the allocation of time on the agenda is the overall amount of time to spend on the call. Fast Company wrote that the ideal meeting length is 15 minutes. I've had some very effective, single-topic conference calls that lasted 10-15 minutes. But for a conference call that is more of a deep-dive or multi-topic, I find the perfect duration to be 45 minutes. Why not an hour? Because then you give all the attendees 15 minutes prior to the next hour, for what will very likely be….. Another conference call!

What about time of day? While conventional wisdom is that morning meetings are best, evidence suggests otherwise. Mornings are bad because people are still commuting and getting settled, and processing a deluge of incoming messages. For a conference call, that means your attendees will be, at best, multi-tasking, but perhaps even still in their cars. Additionally, if you are working with people from different time zones, a morning conference call for you might be a very-early morning conference call for others.

Midday is the best time for conference calls. People are most likely to be in one spot instead of on the move. They are in the groove of work, instead of just getting in or attempting to head home.

As for day of the week, Monday is a very common day for absences, so you may want to avoid those. And if your company or organization has people who travel regularly, take into account their typical travel schedule so everyone isn't calling in from the road or an airport.

Send Reference Materials in Advance

Pre-reads. Perhaps the most ignored concept in organizational culture today!

Pre-reads and reference materials are important and should be sent in advance, as they will allow the participants to get an idea for the conference content and the discussion points. Many people joining an audio conference may benefit from reading materials in advance, and coming up with questions or ideas in their quiet time instead of on-the-fly.

Amazon has a famous rule that all meetings begin with participants silently reading a two-page memo. Then, discussion on the memo topic ensues. That works too.

For business audio conferences and conference calls, providing advance material and pre-reads also lets you set an expectation that people come prepared to present any queries or questions that they may have. This is especially important in a management scenario, where the contributions from the other management team members can be essential to making the right decision. Being able to have input from other members of your team will allow you to make sure that you are presented with as many options as possible, and you have full input from the group. This, in turn, will allow you to make better decisions coming out of the meeting, and decisions that the group is bought-into because they discussed them together.

Alternatively, for an audio conference that is being hosted as an event or teaching opportunity, providing reference materials in advance is just as important. Sometimes, the listeners that you are presenting to will not understand the topic that you are discussing. As such, for these people, providing reference materials in advance can be of huge benefit. Sending out information that people can consult prior to the event will allow listeners to refresh their knowledge of the topic in question or otherwise educate themselves about the nature of your talk. This, in turn, will allow them to understand the topic of the audio conference better while also making sure that they have ample time to come up with any questions and queries that they might want to ask following the main talks.

Reference materials can come in many different formats. Commonly, people hosting audio conferences will send out powerpoint content and charts to help support their presentations. Furthermore, links to online resources which can allow for reading around the subject matter may be useful for people who have a more limited knowledge of the specific niche for which you are referring to.

My favorite reference material or pre-read is a simple one-page write-up that gets to the point quickly, and outlines the decision or call-to-action that is needed. This document can also be an agenda with content embedded in it.

But Assume People Can't See the Reference Materials!

Giving out reference material in advance of your event is important, and should be a habit everyone has. However, I want you to be ready for anything and able to facilitate the best conference calls possible. Just because you sent out reference material does not mean people have read this content. Indeed, your audio talk should still be tailored in such a way as to cater for people who have not had a chance to refer to the reference materials. This will allow you to make sure that everyone who tunes in to the audio conference will have a chance of understanding the topic of your talk—irrelevant of whether or not they have an existing experience and understanding of the content area.

This is more important when conducting client or customer business via conference call. You do not want to admonish them for not having read the pre-reads. On an internal call with your team, it is a little easier to have a zero-tolerance policy.

It may be worth considering in advance why people may not see the reference materials. Sometimes, people are simply too busy in their day to day lives to be able to read extensive amounts of content; as such, you should make sure that your reference materials include both detailed explanations and brief overviews of the topic, to give every listener the best chance of checking out the reference materials.

Perhaps you set the call for a time when everyone is on their commute. If so, consider a better time for future calls.

Furthermore, you may also want to think about the complexity of the topic and the reference materials, and tailor the nature of the reference materials to your target audience; if the audio conference is being presented to passionate students, for example, then you may need to provide more background knowledge in your reference material and simplify the language slightly to ensure the message is conveyed; and vice versa.

Whatever you do, navigate through the call like the emcee of a talk show, and make it easy for people to follow the discussion even if they don't have the pre-read in front of them.

Develop Your "Phone Voice", and Have a Better Vocal Range

In the next chapter, I spend a little more time on how to improve your timbre and vocal range, which is so important for an effective conference call participant. When it comes to presenting as part of an audio conference, your voice takes the place of your body for all of the nonverbal communication. Indeed, a key limitation of audio conferences is that listeners cannot see you and your body language to help them understand the nature of your communication. Furthermore, the lack of body language may also make it harder for your listeners to concentrate and focus; as such, you will need to work on your vocal range and presenting abilities to make sure that your listeners remain engaged by your talk.

Think about a radio DJ on a morning talk show. They have a clear, pleasant voice to listen to. They vary their pitch, almost excessively, so people can tell when they are making certain points. And they at times go fast, at other times slow. They are not afraid of a little silence.

As part of working on your voice, you need to create your "phone voice". This will allow your words and sentences to have more impact, and you can have a tone that people are interested in following. Moreover, it will also guarantee that your listeners can hear and understand the point that you are getting across -- something that is easier to do when you are in person with them. Indeed, improving your natural vocal range is an incredibly important skill that all audio conferencing speakers need to work on. Best of all, it will translate to all of your communications in any setting.

Insist that People Mute Themselves When Not Talking

Muting your mic, computer, or phone when you are not talking should be a cardinal rule for all conference calls.

For people who aren't talking at any one time during the conference call, it is important to mute their own mics, mobile devices and anything that picks up audio. This is something that a lot of people don't even consider, however, it is something that you should make sure to prioritize when you are leading—or joining—a call. Don't be afraid to repeat it at the outset of every call.

Even if someone is staying quiet, the background noise from their location (for example, traffic in the background, the sound of the kettle whistling as a cup of coffee is made, or even innocent breathing or coughing) can be quite distracting for other members of the conference call who are trying to focus on what is being said.

And yes, I have been on calls when people use the toilet without muting their phone.

There are few things that are more distracting than background noise during a conference call. As such, it is essential that you mute your device if you are not in a speaking position at that point in time; this will allow you to continue to hear the call and the content being discussed, however, will prevent your connection from disturbing other actively talking members of the conference call.

If you are leading a conference call, remind people at the outset to mute. If you get noise from someone who has not muted, stop the call and remind folks to mute. Many people don't realize just how loud their background noise can be.

Don't be afraid to make sure your listeners are ready to mute their devices, and remind them early and often. It is far better to call someone out in the first few minutes of a meeting for not being muted, than to have the entire group have to tolerate their background noise for 30 or 60 minutes.

This rule goes for you as well! When you are not speaking, be on mute. Make this habit second nature. A little-known feature of Zoom and some of the other apps is that you can actually setup your default to always join calls on mute. This creates a situation where you need to take action in order to be heard, rather than the opposite -- having to remember to take action to be muted.

Consider General Etiquette

When participating in a conference call, there are a number of different etiquette points that you should consider. It is important that you work to ensure you are talking in line with the norms for that particular group, in order to avoid infuriating any of the fellow listeners or speakers on the call (or even your own audience, if you are hosting the call).

There are a few things that break the "conference call etiquette" rules, and some of these are already explained above—namely, excessive background noise, or not being on mute when not speaking. In addition, make sure that you are aware of some other common conference call etiquette rules so that the call goes without issue.

At the outset of most calls, you will want to clearly introduce yourself to your fellow listeners or to your audience. This is a simple thing but helps other people recognize you. Nobody likes lurkers. The cutoff point for introductions is somewhere around 15-20 people. Above that, introductions can be cumbersome and too time-consuming.

If you are the leader of a regular, standing call that has 25 or fewer participants, consider doing a roll call. It can be a very quick run-through of who you expect on the call, with a simple "here" for folks who are present. It should just take a minute.

If you are attending a conference call in a professional scenario, such as with new clients or customers, introducing your business or your role may also help other people understand your comments thanks to the context that this can provide. Insist that introductions be a part of the outset of the meeting -- it is always good to be crystal clear who else is on the call. If you have multiple people from your organization on the call, cleanly handoff from one person to the other for introductions, so that people are not talking over each other.

It might go without saying, but be present and stay engaged. What is the point of joining a conference call if you don't listen? Try not to multitask, follow the conversation, and contribute when useful.

In addition to this, it is also important to employ general conversational etiquette. Don't talk over other people, and if multiple people are talking at once, it is vital that you step back and allow others to voice their own opinions so as to keep the atmosphere calm and professional, during the call.

Simply put: be courteous to other conference call audience members or speakers. This will help to ensure that the audio conference runs without arguments or distractions, and will allow all listeners to get the most from the call that they possibly can. In short, you will just get more done if you have some simple ground rules that everyone follows.

It is only shallow people who do not judge by appearances

—Oscar Wilde

How to be a Pro
at Video Conferences

All of the points I made for audio conference calls can apply to video conferences as well. But with video conferences, there is obviously another layer of skill and complexity involved – the fact that you are now a visual presence too, not just an audio voice.

Video conferences are very similar to audio conferences, however, they come with their own benefits and drawbacks. They require more effort on the part of the attendees and speakers. However, in many scenarios, they can also give a more personal experience and an opportunity to relationship-build that doesn't exist with a pure conference call.

First things first, from a technology perspective, video conference calls require far more bandwidth than an audio conference call. This is an important fact to consider, as failing to account for this can result in a poor quality video stream which may impact on the professionalism of the conference call itself.

A successful video conference will be one which is not interrupted continually by lagging streams and unclear image quality; as such, before getting started with video conferencing, it is important to test the video quality. In general, it can be expected that the requirements for video conferencing will be approximately 1 Mbps per viewer, for high definition content and live streaming. This is 10 - 15 times the bandwidth needed for an audio call. If this requirement for fast internet connectivity and a generous amount of bandwidth is unlikely to be met, an audio conference or a smaller audience size may be a better option to consider.

In addition, it is worth considering that video conferences are also more demanding on the people involved. Audio conferences are great in the fact that you can do them from anywhere. And wearing anything. If a person doesn't want to, they don't need to clean up much for the meeting. Moreover, audio conference calls allow a speaker or listener to participate from a comfortable location—wherever they might feel most at home. By contrast, this is not the case for video conferences, which require a more professional appearance and location.

It is important to note that video conference technology, and the associated apps, are evolving at a very fast pace. One tangible example is that when I first wrote this book, I never recommended that people use their computer's microphone as their audio intake device. In just a few short months, both the hardware and the app software improved enough so that using your computer is often a great option -- as long as you are working from a quiet location. The point is that technology is improving by the month.

Either way, video conferencing doesn't need to be hard to master. With some time and concentration, you will be able to learn how to make the most of your video conferencing for both you and your business.

Have an Agenda

Yes, I mentioned this in the conference call section. But it bears repeating.

Having an agenda is equally important for both video and audio conferences. In fact, some people might even argue that agendas are even more important in the case of video conferences.

During an audio conference, there is no live image being streamed; in effect, this means that you will be attending a group phone call. However, video conferences are far closer to real conferences in that you will be able to see your fellow audience members or other speakers; this can mean that you will be far more likely to get distracted and go off on a tangent during a video conference. Video conferences are far more personal than an audio conference and can have a friendly atmosphere, which means that it is easy to get distracted and begin discussing topics and points which were not originally going to be part of the discussions.

Having an agenda is important in order to prevent your meeting from going off the rails. An agenda will help you to work out a plan for the conference and will list all points of discussion so that you don't accidentally forget a point in all of the excitement. Furthermore, a good agenda will allow you to ensure that you are sticking to time so that the conference does not overrun—which is something that is common when conferences have a lot of topics to discuss, especially in the case where the chosen topics are ones which are controversial or are otherwise easy to continue talking about.

Invest in Quality Video Gear

For audio conferences, having top quality audio technology is essential—but video conferences take things a step further. Indeed, although having premium quality audio gear is imperative, you will also need to make sure that your video equipment is also working well.

I discuss my recommended virtual call equipment in a later section of this book. If you want the punch line now, I can tell you that the best all-around webcam for zoom meetings right now is the Logitech Brio. It is a great combination of picture quality, focus on the speaker (versus the background) and value. I love it, and you can find it here on Amazon.

Video equipment can come in a vast array of different qualities. When hosting or attending a video conference, it is essential that your video gear is able to capture high quality pictures so that other conference attendees will be able to see you in crystal clear quality. Failing this, you may find that your video gear produces a video which either lags or is otherwise not overly high quality, which may impact on your professionalism and may result in poor impressions from your audience and/or peers, too. And, after all—you want to be making a great impression, especially if you are attending a video conference on behalf of a business.

The distraction factor of poor video equipment or bad bandwidth is huge.

Before you head out and purchase new technology, though, it is worth thinking about your current tech. Video technology doesn't need to be fancy, necessarily; in fact, you might find that your current devices already come with good enough camera and video recording technology, built in. A lot of modern tablet devices and laptops have incredibly powerful cameras, and this is especially the case for the type of laptop you may already be using for your work.

In addition, there are numerous different conferencing apps that allow for video conferencing between team members to be easy, and help you look and sound good. For example, Zoom has a great feature called Touch Up My Appearance which smoothes skin tones and makes you look better. Get to know your app, and the features it might offer.

Test Your Equipment Before Your First Call, and In-Between Calls and Meetings!

I am surprised by how many people do not explore and test their video equipment before their calls. I have seen many calls where attendees spend the first 10 minutes trying to figure out the technology. It doesn't have to be that way.

People who have never experienced a fault with their video equipment will forget to consider that preparation and testing is one of the keys to success. It is always important to routinely test your video gear to make sure that it is working well. Faults can develop without much warning, and in some cases, there may be no warning until just before call time that your camera isn't working or your bandwidth is overloaded. This may mean that you will be caught with suboptimal video equipment at the start of a video conference, and this can really impact on the overall experience.

When it comes to video conferencing, there are few things that break conference etiquette more than your video stream not working right, or "hiccuping" on the call.. This can be incredibly distracting if you are an attendee of the conference, and if you are a speaker, it can clearly be a major problem!

The good news is that you can prepare and test your equipment whenever you want.

Testing your equipment should include more than just your video tech! A lot of people forget to check their internet connectivity, even if they have checked the condition of their video gear. This can sometimes mean that a person's internet connection may not be adequate for video conferencing— which requires a powerful internet connection—and they may begin to experience connectivity issues early on during the video conference. Luckily, testing your internet connection before the call doesn't need to be hard; there are plenty of internet speed testing software solutions available on the internet for free that you can try to make sure your device will be able to handle the strain of video conferencing.

When you are testing your equipment, learn how to turn off the video when needed. It needs to become second nature.

In Zoom, you can easily do this with a click of the "Video" button in the bottom left corner. With other apps, there is a similar feature to turn off the video. If worse comes to worse, you can turn off or cover your camera with your hardware. There will be times when someone enters your room, you need to take care of something, or you simply want a quick stretch break. Better to turn off the video for a minute than to do all of that on camera.

In the event your video feed begins to fail during a video call, go off-video right away to see if that helps. The bandwidth required to carry a video connection is much higher than that for audio only. If you find yourself freezing or becoming glitchy, there is a good chance that turning video off for a moment will help.

Think About Your Background

I promise you that the first thing people will do when you join their video meeting is look at your background. It is human nature. What does your office look like? Which room are you in? What is on your wall?

Before joining a video conference, make sure that your background is suitable. Many people just blur their background, or use a fake background supplied by the conferencing app. That is just fine, and in many cases a good answer. However, studies have shown that people in a virtual meeting prefer to see an actual background as long as it is distraction-free.

It is best to have 2-3 go-to backgrounds. One might be your home office, with some shelving, books, or pictures in the background. One of my colleagues keeps an acoustic guitar hangiing from the wall, which is a nice, interesting, clean touch. The other backgrounds might be a blurred background, and perhaps your company logo. Use each in settings where they make the most sense, and be able to easily toggle between them.

The ideal background for a professional video conference call is one which is plain and professional. A lot of people choose a simple white background, without excessive imagery or furnishings in the way. The only exception to this might be for a video conference on a specific topic, where having relevant props in the background could help to set the scene; for example, for medical conferences, a great place to hold the conference (if the space is available) is actually in your consulting room.

By contrast, if you are hosting or participating in a more general conference, any background is suitable. For regular, internal company meetings, a good background is a simple wall, or a wall with some photos or a whiteboard. Don't worry about impressing people -- the goal is actually to *not* draw attention to your background.

Beware of windows and light. A window might be nice to have in your workspace, but a bright light coming into an otherwise darker office will actually create a glare and take the focus off of your face. If anything, the light should be in front of you. The rule is that the light should generally be in your eyes (but not to the point where you squint.)

Keep in mind that any movement in the video frame will affect bandwidth, whether it is you waving your hand, a ceiling fan, people milling about in the next room over, or the visible branches of a tree blowing outside. To preserve the bandwidth for what matters most -- your head and your voice -- try to minimize this visual "noise" that can consume resources.

Your desk should also be a consideration. On the whole, the other conference attendees won't be able to see a large amount of your desk; it is likely that they will only be able to see the space directly in front of your screen. However, even this space can get cluttered easily. Try to make sure the only thing visible on the screen is you and the background; this means removing, or at least moving to the side, any cups, stacks of paper, and the like.

In addition to thinking about what people will see behind you, you may also want to think about what you will be able to see during the video conference. In other words, what distractions will be around you during the video conference call? It is incredibly easy to get distracted during a conference call, especially when you are not actively talking; however, it is always important to keep your full focus on the camera during the conference. Otherwise, if you are distracted, you won't be paying full attention; not only is this unprofessional, but you may also end up missing questions or, if you are a listener, miss some incredibly important information. So, when choosing a location for your video conference call, try to choose one that has a suitable background without risking distraction on your part. Turn off the television, stop multitasking, and make sure that nothing will be more interesting than what is going on, on screen.

Some web meeting applications provide the option of an artificial background, such as a sunset, city scene, or aquarium with fish. You can also customize a background, and I have seen many people create a customized, professional background, perhaps with a company logo behind them. This is a great option if you are unsure of your real background, or calling-in from somewhere such as a car or airport. I love this functionality, just don't choose a background that will distract from the meeting. Busy is not better.

Keep Your Camera Stable

You want your video camera to be in a stable, stationary place. If you are using your laptop or computer, it is as simple as setting it on a table or desk. Same goes for a video camera on a stand or tripod, if you use one.

Avoid having a camera that is moving around, either with a phone in your hand, a tablet that you are holding, or a laptop on our lap. I call this the Blair Witch Project effect (dating me to a late 90s film) where your entire world, to the others on the call, is shaking and shifting. I was recently on a video call where one attendee had their laptop (which included their camera) on their lap, and they had a nervous tick where they rapidly twitched their ankle up-and-down. It caused the entire video picture of them to shake, and they had no idea they were doing it.

It is fine for you to move around slightly, especially for comfort or dramatic effect, but avoid the camera being what is moving.

Dress and Look the Part

It doesn't take much work to dress professionally for a video conference, so why wouldn't you?

When joining an audio call, you won't need to think about what you look like; though it is good practice to make sure that you dress for the occasion, in order to help you get into the right professional mindset. Research suggests that the clothes you are wearing can affect your emotions and make you feel powerful or otherwise.

There is technically nothing to stop you from joining an audio conference call in your pajamas while eating your breakfast! However, this is not the case for people who are attending a video conference call; for them, appearance and presentation is naturally a far more important aspect.

Tidy up. Brush your hair and make yourself presentable. Straighten your collar and tie, if applicable, and make sure that you are neat and professional. This is key. With audio conference calls, you can get away without putting so much emphasis on how you look, but this is naturally not the case for a video conference call.

When choosing your outfit for video conferencing, consider an outfit that is neutral in color. Try to stay away from especially bright or bold colors, in order to not draw all of the attention to yourself. Blacks, whites and stripes are important colors to avoid; blacks and whites often just look like a "blob" on the screen, and stripes can take on a psychedelic hue. If you can, choose instead a dark gray, blue, or any other sort of solid color that won't create a distraction.

Solid colors are best, because the camera resolution can easily process a solid. If you wear a patterned top, it can create the "wavy line effect" where your top will be moving out-of-focus the entire time. A solid color is best, and preferably something that does not blend in to the background. In other words, if the paint on your wall behind you is tan, don't wear a tan top.

For guys, I always suggest wearing a collared shirt. It is easy to do, and makes you look more professional. You can be the judge on how formal you need to look based on the audience you are talking with. For women, a solid, bold color is a good choice, and keep jewelry simple and basic.

Many of the professional men and women I know keep a couple "video outfits" nearby, so they can throw them on with little notice and be ready for the camera. I keep a couple nice, solid polo shirts for casual meetings, and a couple solid-color button-down shirts for more formal meetings. I even keep a blazer-style jacket that I can throw on if I am presenting to a group of dressed-up folks. All are on hangers within a 10 second walk of my video setup.

For both men and women, pay attention to if you have oily, shiny skin, and take appropriate measures before the meeting. For guys, know that stubble is even more noticeable on a video call than it is in person. Shave.

If you are using Zoom, there is a great feature called "Improve my Appearance" that can be found in the Video Settings dropdown from the Video button. You will find it in the bottom left corner of the screen. By using this feature, you can soften any rough spots on your complexion, and improve your overall tone. It does not compensate for bad lighting (we will get to that next) but you might as well use it.

Think About Lighting

There is a reason that television studios invest so much in lighting. It does wonders for the production value of any video.

As well as considering your background, surroundings, and dress code, lighting ranks up there as one of the important things to pay attention to. No one wants to be joining a conference call in the dark; with that being said, a conference call with a single bright light overhead can also make you feel uncomfortable, as if you are about to be interrogated! The best compromise is to make the best use of natural light as possible, and always try to use gentle side lighting to create the best environment.

I have been on calls where very high-level executives have horrible lighting on their calls. It makes them look like amateurs.

If you have a window or natural lighting, that is best. Face the window, or at least have the natural light shining on you from either side, preferably toward the front. It can make a huge difference.

Don't Hover Over Your Laptop—Eye Level is Best

A mistake that a lot of people make when they are getting started with video conferencing is to hover over their laptop or video recording device, so that they are looking down at the camera. This is not a good look for video conferencing, it appears to other attendees that you are starting at them down in a hole. Instead, make sure that you are looking directly at the camera. The other participants don't want to stare up your nostrils -- having a camera at even, eye level is best.

Having the right camera angle will add to your professionalism and will help your viewers or peers focus on the topic at hand, and not the odd angle of the camera (which can feel unnerving for many). Not to mention, some camera angles can be incredibly unflattering—in the nicest possible way, not many people want to be looking up someone else's nostrils during what should be a serious and professional video conference. Body wants to stare at your ceiling behind you.

Avoid Talking Through Your Computer (Unless you augment with headphones)

I suspect this advice will change in coming editions of this book, as the computer and laptop mic and audio quality is finally improving. At the time of this writing, though, I would caution against your computer or laptop being your primary audio device.

Some people with especially good internet connections, and latest generations computers, can potentially get away with talking into their computer. In fact, several of the leading virtual meeting apps assume you will use your computer for audio and make it a little complicated to connect via phone. However, on the whole, your computer's mic and speaker are often inferior. Talking through the computer, especially on an older model or in a workspace with background noise, is one of those habits that people find especially annoying, and this is true for both audio and video conferencing alike. As such, it is important to be aware of this during your first few conference calls.

If you want to use your computer as your primary audio connection, I recommend plugging a quality pair of headphones with a noise-canceling mic into the headphone jack on your computer. Or, if your computer is capable of a bluetooth audio connect, you can use earbuds or other wireless headphones.

Your computer audio is getting bandwidth leftovers from the video that is contributing to your virtual meeting. As a result, it can be severely compromised. Instead, I recommend dialing-in to the conference with your phone, preserving the bandwidth for your video stream. If you do this, be sure to marry your phone presence with your video presence, a feature most good meeting apps give you when you dial-in.

Act Like a TV News Anchor

You don't have to reinvent the wheel when it comes to video meetings. Some people have been doing it for decades. They are called news anchors.

TV news anchors are professionals in terms of addressing an audience through video, and if you are a little worried about your own video conferences then you may want to take a page out of their books! News anchors on TV use a number of different tactics to ensure viewer engagement and you, too, can use these during your own video conferencing attempts!

First, it is important to keep eye contact in the camera area. Learn to love that camera. That is who you are talking to, and you should attempt to carry on a conversation with the camera using the facial expressions, head movement, and eye contact that you would in a conversation with another live human being. Reporters and news anchors are good at this -- tilting their head, and using good eye contact but not so good that it is an intense death glare. When you are speaking to someone, they are not on your computer screen, they are in the camera.

Second, it is important to speak at a speed that is appropriate for the viewers; study how news anchors speak and act, and then use these mannerisms during your own video conferences to make sure that you are engaging for your audience!

News anchors also use plenty of voice inflection, pauses and silence, smiles, eyebrow movements, and head tilts as part of their repertoire. Study your favorite news anchor and copy them -- it works!

Beware of the Jokes

Jokes and other such bantar are usually best left for physical meetings. Though good fun, both of the aforementioned generally just don't land as well in a video or audio conference call. This is, in part, due to the fact that judging body language can be harder through a conference call than in person. Plus, with people on mute, a joke delivered with little audience response can feel like a resounding thud.

Leave the jokes for the time being and remember to use a friendly but more professional persona while talking through video conference; otherwise, you might find your joke backfiring when it doesn't go down as well as you had expected. Remain calm, composed, and focused.

Smile!

While jokes are risky, smiling is not. I onced received feedback from a peer that I needed to smile more on my video conferences. I played back a recent video meeting that had been recorded, and sure enough. My eyebrows were furrowed and my face was frowned the whole time. I was covering a professional topic and my words were perfect, but my face looked like I was telling someone their dog had died.

Remember to smile. It makes a huge difference on how you are perceived, and is so easy. Remember, too, that you smile with your eyes. Don't furrow your eyebrows like I did. Rather, show a face on the camera that is open, inquisitive, and positive.

Remember—practice makes perfect! No one can expect to be a pro at video conferencing immediately, but by following our tips and studying how the professionals tackle the matter, you will surely be able to find strategies and tricks to allow you to work at your best in front of the camera.

On Camera or Off?

Decided if you should be on camera or off defines the dynamic for any video meeting.

On-camera meetings are definitely more effective for 1:1 discussions, and it is not even close. While it is not quite the same as being across the table from each other, it is a big step better than just looking at someone's name or picture. You can read their face, and see their general state (frenzied, relaxed, sick, etc.) which adds a major human element to the meeting.

Being off camera can work if you are mainly sharing materials, because the materials will take center stage on the screen. As I discuss later, being off-camera also reduces Zoom fatigue.

I recommend having a norm of being on-camera, and saying so. A mix of on or off-camera people gives a vibe that some are proverbially "phoning it in." But if the intent of the meeting is to analyze trends or edit a document, it is ok to be off.

If you are trying to make a good impression on a client or coworkers, err on the side of being on camera.

Facilitating the Meeting Technology -- If you are the Host

For those who will be hosting virtual meetings frequently -- such as a manager, a sales professional, or an educator, it is important to become just as skilled at hosting a virtual meeting as joining one as an attendee.

The specifics of how to host a virtual meeting may depend on the application you are using -- Zoom gets much of the press, but there are many others. A good host is familiar with the features, and minimizing the toggling and downtime associated with wrestling with software. Here are a few tips for improving your meeting facilitation.

1. Be the first one to the meeting. This involves looking at your schedule and making sure you are not booked wall-to-wall for the day. If you are the host of a meeting, try to be the first one there. "Open up" the room, and make sure everything is set to your liking. Welcome people as they join.

2. Clarify the ground rules early. Even if you have said them before, make sure the "code of conduct" is known to everyone. Do you want people to be on mute when not speaking? Do you expect everyone to have video enabled? How do you want people to use any chat features within the app?

3. Know where your host controls are. As host, you can often doing things like share your screen, push a document out to the attendees, or mute a participant whose background noise is distracting and is too oblivious to realize they are not on mute. You can also hide non-video participants from the gallery screen, so that an empty box does not take up useful screen space. These are features that you will have to use at some point, so make it second nature when the time comes to use them.

4. Know the difference between sharing your screen, and sharing a window. Most apps let you specify if you share a particular window or your entire desktop screen. 90% of the time, you should just share a window. If you share your screen, participants see everything – your incoming IMs, the other programs you have open, etc.

5. When the meeting concludes, end the virtual meeting immediately. Most apps keep a virtual meeting open until the host officially closes the meeting. This can create some awkwardness if the meeting is over but people are not yet off camera or logged-out. The problem is solved if you, as host, formally close out the meeting in your app as soon as the meeting has concluded.

A Request

If you like this book so far, or think it could be a valuable reference for others, consider leaving a review. I would appreciate it! Reviews help others decide if this book can help them with their virtual meetings.

You can leave that review here on Amazon, where you found this book.

"For the things we have to learn before we can do them, we learn by doing them."

—Aristotle

Techniques to Improve Your Call Skills

I have worked with a number of people over the years on improving their presentation skills, meeting facilitation capabilities, and other communication skills. As with anything, communication is something that *will* improve if you work at it. 100% chance.

The same principles apply to improving your video and audio conference call skills. You can perform better, be clearer, and have more impact if you build your abilities.

Why don't more people view the virtual meeting as a skill to be honed and developed, just like standing in front of a room giving a speech? I'm not sure. Perhaps the fact that it is a phone or a camera is a bit disarming, and people assuming they have it covered. Maybe folks don't want to admit that they get jittery on calls or wish they were more concise and clearer.

There are some hacks you can use to improve your video and conference skill ability. By the way, these all assume that you read the last chapter, and understand the best practices for conducting and participating in virtual meetings.

Prepare

Good preparation is underrated for many activities. People who prepare for meetings and presentations do better than if they had not. The same can be said for virtual meetings. You should carve-out time to prepare just as you would an in-person presentation, perhaps even more since this might be a new channel for you.

Too often, preparation is left to the five minutes prior to a meeting. Resist the urge to procrastinate and cram.

If you are the presenter, understand the points you want to make, how you plan to navigate from topic to topic, and how to manage the time you have. Have a strong opening that fits the situation, but one that clearly gets people listening and engaged from the start. Don't forget to prepare on the technology -- if presenting on a video conference is not second nature to you, for example, you may want to spend a little time in the video application you will use to understand the controls and features.

If you are not presenting, still prepare. Be sure to read any pre-reads. Know the subject, come prepared with your input and questions, and know how to use the technology.

Find Your Style

When it comes to virtual meetings, the best presentation style is the one that fits you best. It is not one-size-fits-all. Take some time to figure out what the right tone and tempo is for you. It might not be the exact same as if you were in-person, especially if you are a presenter who often relies on nonverbal communication or spontaneous back and forth, both of which are harder to do virtually.

Experiment with techniques not only for your delivery and speaking, but also with your props and office setup. For video meetings, I like to have two monitors that I can glance at in front of me. The first has the others who are in my video conference, along with any content being projected. I consider this my meeting site. The second, larger monitor often has the points I want to make while I am speaking, in a very large font on a document. I can glance over to it without swiveling my head too far, and quickly remember my next key point when talking.

I also like to have a simple yellow notepad and pen on my desk, so I can take important notes on what is being said, or a point that I want to make later. I prefer the notepad over typing on my computer for a couple reasons: First, my two computers already have their "jobs" during a virtual meeting and I hate to deviate from that. Second, I am a big believer that if you are on video, you look more engaged to others if you are jotting notes with a pen than if you are typing on your computer.

These are just examples, there are many other style points you can develop with practice. Find a system that works, and double down on it.

Train Your Voice

On a conference call, your voice is the only point of intersection you have with your audience. On a video call, they can see your face or materials, but you are still much more reliant on the quality of your voice than you would be in-person.

A famous and often-quoted study from the 1970s suggested that communication is 7% verbal (what you say), 38% voice tone, and 55% body language. On a conference call, there is obviously zero body language. On a video conference, there might be a little body language, but it is highly-compromised.

That leaves you with your voice. Voice tone is underrated as a communication technique, and it becomes even more important when you are doing virtual meetings.

I am not a voice coach, and I am not qualified to give any type of voice lessons, but you can find many good voice coaches online, many of whom make their sessions available for free on Youtube or other platforms. It is absolutely worth spending time on these, finding your best voice.

I find that there are three important elements of voice training for virtual meetings that a good (virtual) coach can help you with.

First, breathing. Controlling your breathing is everything. Just ask a singer who relies on vocal power and range, knowing how to breathe is more complicated than it sounds. Being able to take deep breaths from your diaphragm and release them in a controlled manner can have a profound impact on your voice quality. Additionally, knowing when and how to breathe just before you are to speak and be the difference between stumbling into your first minute of talking, or starting with complete engagement from your audience.

Second, timbre. Your voice timbre is unique your own, and the more that you can have a clear voice in a comfortable range for you, the more impactful you will be from an audio perspective. Timbre takes advantage of finding the natural range for your vocal chords, and making sure you have your lungs, nose, and mouth working in concert for the best sound product. Opera singers spend years refining their timbre -- it pays for professionals to devote a little time to it as well. Trying to interject points on a conference call when you have a stuffy, scratchy, or laboring voice doesn't have the impact that it would if your voice was clearer and stronger.

Third, range. Because of the lack of nonverbal and physical communication when you are on a call or virtual meeting, you need to be able to make more points with your voice tone. If you are at a meeting presenting a question for the group to think about, you naturally do things with your eyes and arms that suggest you are posing a question. When you don't have those tools available, you need to rely on your voice. That is just one example, but there are many others. Work on range, and what feels like voice exaggeration to you might simply feel engaging to those who you are meeting with.

Record Yourself, and Then Study It

Recording yourself while speaking, if you have not ever done it, is a productive if not slightly frightening experience. Whether you expect to be doing more audio or video meetings, you can record yourself in that mode and listen to or watch the playback. What you find will be eye-opening.

I started listening to recordings of myself after hiring a coach to get my presentation skills to the next level. He shared with me that for all the best speakers out there, they study their own performances. Even if you don't have a goal of being a world-renowned speaker, you can employ this technique and vastly improve.

Recording yourself and then studying your performance is not of the most underused benefits of video (and audio) conferences. Professional athletes study their game film constantly. Why don't we?

If you are like me, if you watch or listen to yourself, you will notice filler words, throat-clearing, phrasing that doesn't make sense, and either more or less silence than you expected to hear. You will also find that what you thought was a convincing conversation with good vocal range actually comes across as more monotone or flat than you thought it would.

Most video meeting applications provide the ability for you to do a dry run and record yourself. Many have a test meeting area, or an option to log-in as if you are in a meeting, only you are the only one. In a pinch, you can simply record yourself on your phone and play it back. Listen and look for your habits and tendencies, but also your flow. Are you easy to follow? Would someone listening walk away with the same major points you think you are making?

You can also ask to have your actual meetings recorded, which is easy in most web meeting applications, and then listen to the playback later. Hearing or seeing yourself in real action is very useful.

Listen and watch, adjust, and do it again. You <u>will</u> get better.

Get More Repetitions

They say that practice makes perfect. It is as true for virtual meetings as it is for stand-up presentations or other meeting facilitation. The more you get out there and do, the more you will improve.

By doing more virtual meetings, a positive cycle of good things will happen. You will become more confident, you will be better at using your technology, and you will settle on a style that works for you.

If you are in a situation where you just can't get many repetitions, but still want to improve, get creative. You can record yourself as I mentioned above, or you can ask a family member to Facetime with you while you practice presenting via video. For a more real-life feel, ask someone to log-in to the same virtual meeting application that you will be using for your meetings, so you can get a good feel for how the software works.

Deal with Your Nerves

Do you have nerves when you present or speak-up on a video or audience conference call? Welcome to the club.

The nerves that you feel when presenting in person will certainly exist during virtual meetings. Just because the communication channel has changed doesn't mean the nerves go away. It is human nature.

I have found two things that help with my nerves, whether I am doing an in-person presentation or meeting, a conference call, or a video presentation.

First, breathe. Managing your breathing makes a huge difference on your overall level of anxiety. Before joining a conference that I need to present at, I do some 4-7-8 breathing. At least three cycles of 4 counts breathing in, 7 counts of holding my breath, and then 8 counts of breathing out. It calms me down significantly, and helps me get a grip on my nerves.

Continuing with my breathing, I make a point of taking a couple deep breaths before I am about to talk, with nice, full exhales. Then, when it is my turn to go, I take a nice, full breathe, breathe halfway out, and begin. For some reason, it works.

Second, I prepare. My worst presentations -- via video, audio, or in-person -- are when I did not prepare enough. While the first minute of any presentation is a bit anxious, if you prepare, the presentation goes great once you get past the initial adrenaline rush.

Fatigue, discomfort, discouragement are merely symptoms of effort.

—Morgan Freeman

"Zoom Fatigue"

A term was coined during the 2020 COVID-19 crisis, when many people shifted to work-from-home overnight: Zoom fatigue. The theory is that virtual, and especially video, meetings can be extremely helpful at first, but they become tiring very quickly.

Why can a virtual meeting be such a fatiguing activity? There are a few reasons. First, when we are in a virtual meeting, we tend to focus on ourselves -- how we look on camera, if the background is right, etc. If you think about it, those are things we don't do as often when meeting in-person, and we certainly don't focus on our appearance during an audio call. It takes effort.

Second, a virtual meeting requires additional concentration. The channels of intake are lessened, meeting that if you are in an important meeting, you don't have the benefit of reading body language, scanning the room, and sensing the "vibe" of the meeting. Your focus is on one person, or perhaps a presentation being shown, and that channel requires heightening concentration in order to keep up. Your more natural state is taking things in from multiple channels in a very balanced way.

Finally, As the Wall Street Journal pointed out, there is simply an increase in the number of interactions you can have throughout the day when everyone is virtual. That colleague who works in an office 1,000 miles away is normally someone you would see a few times a year, but with virtual meetings you might see him or her daily. If you were in-person with a group of coworkers, you probably would not be scheduling back-to-back-to-back-back meetings, each with about 20 seconds in between. There would at least be breaks. But when you are Zooming, you find yourself in video meetings with many different groups on many different topics. To top it all off, friends might want to have a "virtual happy hour" at the end of it. The number of interactive commitments increases, which can be tiring even for an extravert.

What to do about Zoom Fatigue?

There are a few things you can do to help reduce Zoom fatigue, both for yourself, but also for those who you are asking to join you in meetings.

1. Recognize that Zoom Fatigue is real. The first step is acknowledging that you and your colleagues are not crazy for becoming fatigued by virtual meetings. With that understanding, you can set some ground rules for the group.

2. Take breaks. The main thing that can help combat Zoom fatigue is frequent breaks. If you are scheduling meetings, make sure you build-in breaks between meetings, so people are not going from one virtual meeting to another with no time to move around or attend to other matters. If you are an educator, be cognizant of the next commitment your students have, and allow them several minutes in between. This might be shortening your session, but it will be worth it.

3. Go off video. It can help to not always be on video. I recommend that some calls be setup as audio-only, so that people can get a mental break from being on-camera. For longer calls that are video-enabled, it is perfectly acceptable to hit that "Stop Video" button for few minutes, move around, or simply lean back in your chair. This is made easier if you have a bluetooth headset that allows you to move around.

4. Consider your hardware. While I do not use a standing desk, I know of several trusted colleagues who swear by the utility of being able to stand during virtual meetings. Additionally, consider investing in

a larger desktop pc. If you have a company-issued laptop, or attempt to take virtual meetings on your tablet, you may have to strain to see the conversation. A large-screened computer can make the viewing experience much more relaxed. I have one that I bought used for a fraction of the MSRP, and it's only purpose in my office is to enable my virtual meetings as well as some web browsing.

'I never teach my pupils; I only attempt to provide the conditions in which they can learn.'

—Albert Einstein

A Word for Educators

This book is to be intended for anyone who does virtual meetings in any walk of life, and I try to make the tips and guidance as profession-agnostic as possible. There is one profession that might warrant a special brief chapter: Education.

Teachers who have to use Teams, Zoom, Skype, and other applications to conduct virtual classes encounter their own set of considerations and challenges. Most teachers who I know went into education so they could interact with a class and have direct dialogues with students as they explored topics, or in the case of younger students, helped prepare them to learn.

The advice I give throughout this book absolutely applies to educators. Making sure you have good lighting, or are using your voice intonation effectively are important in any industry. With that said, there are a few specific points that educators should keep in mind as they are conducting virtual classes or guidance discussions.

1. **Set some ground rules**. This is important in any setting, but when you are dealing with a class of students, it is critical. Ground rules regarding attendance, how to interject or ask questions, muting, and use of video are even more important with group of students. Set these rules during the very first class, even if you have to use a good part of that session just to discuss the rules.

2. **Golden Silence is important**. When you are looking for a class to be interactive, with students interjecting ideas and questions, it is

important to have some whitespace in your agenda. A 10 second pause for questions might seem like forever to you, but it could be the difference between a student speaking up or just staying quiet.

3. **Keep the topics short**. If you are looking at the same slide for more than 5-7 minutes, you are probably going to lose people. If you can cover multiple topics, each with a different look and feel (maybe one is group discussion, the next is you covering a handout) you will keep people engaged.

4. **Be nimble with your hosting capabilities**. It is imperative that a teacher is able to easily toggle between sharing a slide, moving into full gallery mode, sharing other handouts, and even project a short video clip, all in the course of one class or session. This requires more work on the part of the teacher, but will create a more engaged class.

5. **Use your app's Whiteboard function, if it offers one**. As of this writing, Zoom and Teams both offer a Whiteboard app or add-on, while GoToMeeting offers a group "Drawing" function, and Google Meets offers a Jamboard feature. These allow you to interactively sketch on the same concept as if it was a whiteboard or chalkboard, which can be particularly useful for subjects like math.

6. **Have the students present**. One of the most critical things you can to do drive interest, variety, and interactivity is to ask the students to present on topics. Presentations don't have to be long -- they can simply be 2 or 3 minute sharing on the subject you are currently studying -- but the variety will add much to your classes. For younger students, an old-fashioned show-and-tell of something they have at home can give the students a chance to build their sharing and speaking skills.

7. **Take care of the hardware necessities**. Periodically remind students (or their parents) to keep their devices charged, especially important as many students use a tablet as their e-learning device of choice.

8. **Consider bandwidth**. If you are in an area that does not offer broad and fast internet coverage, consider making each class available for

viewing asynchronously for several hours after the class. If people have internet but bandwidth can be slow, don't overload it with high-consumption multimedia that won't feed.

9. **Think about security.** Sadly, there are probably who enjoy disrupting classes and meetings with irrelevant or vulgar meeting crashing or "Zoombombing." Use the security features to limit the meeting only to invited participants, and require a password if that is an option. Never post the details of your meeting anywhere where they can be read or downloaded by a stranger.

From a style standpoint, there is one important exception to my normal set of rules that I make for educators. In a business or other work setting, I often advise my readers to minimize the personal distractions that might show up on camera. Your client probably does not want to see your cat, and your coworkers have limited patience for your children interrupting again and again, as cute as they are. If you are talking to professional colleagues, you may want to have the look of conducting the meeting from your home office rather than your kitchen island.

When it comes to an educator dealing with his or her students, I loosen up on this rule.

Students are fascinated by their teachers and the personal lives of those they look up to. To the extent it is appropriate to share some details, and you are comfortable doing so, consider sharing a bit more in a virtual learning setting than you might in a meeting with colleagues. Feel free to take a couple minutes at the beginning of a class to introduce your pet, your spouse, or share an important photo that you keep in your office. This type of sharing on occasion can help you connect with your students and allow them to feel more engaged with you. While it does not replace the relationship that you can build in the classroom, it will make the virtual learning environment a little less cold and transactional.

"To the man who only has a hammer, everything he encounters begins to look like a nail."

—Abraham Maslow

Virtual Meeting Equipment

When it comes to video and audio conferences, equipment quickly becomes part of the conversation. Somebody doing a conference call on inferior equipment immediately stands out as a rookie, and someone who lacks a certain professionalism. Somebody who has equipment that works well, and every time, is viewed as more professional and in some cases more able.

It's not fair, but it is what it is.

Having the right tools doesn't compensate for lack of skill, but rather can help you maximize your potential while working virtually.

The specific product recommendations I make here are dynamic, because the technology market changes so much.

Many of the suggestions below are written with an angle for a home-based worker, but they are equally applicable to those in office or other settings.

With that said, I feel it is important to outline the product concepts that will help you make the most of your virtual work. Here is my guidance, based on having participated in thousands of virtual meetings.

Computer (x2)

I choose not to spend a lot of time writing about your computer or laptop choices, for a couple key reasons.

First, I am not a computer expert. Most people have specific needs regarding the right computer for them, and there are better and more knowledgeable writers on the subject.

Second, I find that most employed workers have a computer issued from their company or organization, so it becomes a bit of a moot point.

I would simply note that there is merit in considering a second computer for your office space. It allows you to easily have multiple screens with different content up at the same time, and a small laptop screen can be a real chore to look at for 8 hours a day. A larger screen can be a nice change of pace.

I have always used my company-issued laptop (they tend to swap mine out every couple years) along with an IMac that has a nice, large screen, setup right next to it. That effective combo makes my home office a place I hardly ever want to leave.

Headphones / Microphone

Choosing the right headphone / mic combo is such an important decision. I believe that most virtual meeting participants who sound awful have no idea they are coming across so poorly. I don't want you to be one of those people.

99% of at-home workers use some type of earphone, a headphone and microphone combination, or their computer mic and speaker. There is nothing worse than holding a phone up to your ear for an hour-long call, and while the speakerphone functionality is OK, is it not nearly as clear as a good headset or set of headphones.

When it comes to using headphones or some type of microphone, you have a few options. I will list them from most common to least.

Wired headphones. A most common headphone / microphone alternative is the wired headphone, but that may be changing shortly as wireless options become the norm. If you go this wired route, just be sure that the microphone is effective and picks-up your voice well.

The headphones that come as standard equipment with most new mobile phones are actually decent in terms of comfort, audio, and microphone quality, but I recommend you go a step further and get something with noise-reduction features. The people you are meeting with will thank you for it.

Some people prefer a higher-end headphone with noise-reduction functionality. Others actually do not like the way the noise cancellation makes their voice sound to them when they are speaking, so they opt for something without noise-cancellation in the headphones. The noise-cancellation on the microphone, however, is a nice feature, allowing your voice to be heard more clearly amidst other sounds when you are speaking. It will make a big difference on how you are received by others.

Know that earphones, and especially the microphones on them, wear out after a period of time. Expect that this will be a piece of equipment you need to repurchase several times. In fact, I recommend always having a good spare on hand. The good news is that you do not need to spend an arm and a leg on these -- you can usually find quality products for less than $50. $100 gets you a great set.

An advantage of the wired headphones is that power charging is not a factor. There is no battery to worry about, unless you go quite high-end. You just plug them in to your phone (or computer) jack, and go.

Airpods, Or Wireless Headphones. Wireless, bluetooth-enabled headphones -- airpods are the most popular -- are coming on strong and might be eclipsing the wired headphone market. Many people prefer the wireless version because -- well -- they don't have cords or wires, and are much more concealed and less cumbersome.

When the wireless headphones first came out, I had two questions. First, do they even have microphones? Second, since they did have microphones, how was the quality?

The products check-out on both counts. Microphone quality is good due to high-tech dual placement on, and most of the products tend to have very good in--ear audio quality with an element of noise cancellation. The other advantage is that they are barely noticeable when you are on video, and in many cases create less distraction than a cord hanging from your face.

With wireless headphones, you don't want to skimp. The sound quality on the other end of the line can really be compromised with the cheaper ones, especially when there is any background noise at all. You will also need to keep them charged, typically in a carrying case that comes with the headphones. Investigate the battery life of the headphones before purchasing, because if the battery is drained, a wireless headphone flat-out doesn't work. Charging is not a factor with most wired headphones.

In addition to a good battery life, the other feature to look for is noise cancellation. Noise reduction or cancelation should be a feature both for the audio portion in your ears, but also for the microphone. A good set of headphones will minimize any noise coming from wind, traffic, or ambient noise in your space.

Computer Audio. For most, using the audio functionality on your computer or laptop is a good option, as long as you have a new model computer. Some of the mics and speakers on older computers are not very good, but newer ones have come a long way.

Around 2019 or 2020 is a good cutoff point, generally speaking. Computers built before then are often lacking. Computers built after that time, broadly, are much better in their audio quality – both for output and intake.

Just know that your computer audio competes for bandwidth with all the other apps your computer might be using. Because of that, if you find yourself with shaky internet bandwidth, consider dialing-in with your phone and using the computer for video only.

Headset. If you want to look the part of a remote worker, the headset (not to be confused with headphones) is for you. A good headset looks a bit like those people on commercials who are taking calls at a call center -- it usually fits over your head, has one or two earphones, and a boom to speak into.

The advantages of a headset are the audio quality -- it is second to none -- and comfort. These headsets are usually built for workers who will be on calls from the moment they arrive at work until the moment they leave, so they are designed with comfort in mind. They also have excellent background noise canceling on the microphone, so that the person on the other end is less likely to hear sounds that are not intended to be picked-up.

The disadvantages of a headset are that they are single purpose -- you would really only use them for work calls -- and that they are highly-conspicuous on a video call. Sometimes, you prefer for your head in the video to not be covered with a big, wraparound headset.

A Tip: If you are unsure what you will sound like to your listeners, or want to make sure that the clarity is what you think it will be, just leave yourself a voicemail and then listen to it. You will quickly determine if the call quality will be what you need, or if you need to find a Plan B. Additionally, most good web meeting applications have a test site where you can do a video and audio check before the actual live meeting.

Camera

You might be tempted to use the integrated video camera on your laptop or computer, or the camera feature on your phone. If you are going to do any regular volume of video conferencing, I highly suggest investing in an external camera.

A good external camera, as of this writing, will give you HD resolution of 1080p or more. Compare that with 720p in the typical laptop, which doesn't seem so low but it is quite grainy. When everyone in a video meeting is on an HD camera, and one person shows up on 720p, it is easy to see who the low-def one is.

The other great feature of an external camera, in addition to the HD resolution, is that it will automatically detect and adjust the lighting for you. Even if you are in a low-light condition, a good camera will make the most of what you have and allow the viewers to see your face, expressions, and reduce any glare from random lights.

They are much smaller than you might think. A good external camera might be 4 inches wide by an inch tall. A stand, if you get one, will take up a little more space.

You can spend a lot on cameras -- some even will follow you around the room as you move. Those rotating cameras are great for team huddle rooms where different people might speak at different times, but they are overkill for the home office. You can get a good external camera for the single user for under $100.

I recommend adding a video camera stand for $15 to $35. It will allow you to adjust the camera angle, height, and orientation very easily. If you affix the camera to your laptop or computer, the typical default option, you will be limited on the various angles and directions you can use with your camera.

The Logitech Brio is a great all-around camera right now for 99% of remote workers. It is here on Amazon.

Desk - Standup or Sitting?

The decision on which desk to use will probably be a factor of several considerations, your budget and office design constraints among them. It is hard to recommend a one-size-fits-all desk, because everyone has a different personal preference.

The advantage of a standing desk, when it comes to virtual meetings, is that you can obviously move around easier while you talk. It can also look quite natural to be presenting on a videoconference while standing, and you might feel more at ease if you are typically a stand-up presenter. Additionally, many people like to move around while on a conference call, pace while they think, etc.

The bottom line is that, if it is your preference, there are ways to not be tethered to your desk while doing virtual meetings. Find the setup that works for you, your budget, and your space.

Lighting

Lighting is an underrated part of a video conference. Good lighting can make you appear natural, easy-to-see, and perhaps even better looking than you do in real life! Poor lighting will make you look like an amateur. Inadequate lighting causes your facial expressions to be unnoticed, and in some cases the lighting itself can actually be a distraction.

The worst lighting is either a dark environment overall, or a dark environment near the camera with lots of light behind the person who is on camera. The former will be just plain dark, while the latter will make you look like you are a shadow, and the other attendees will barely be able to figure out what you actually look like.

As with so many things, nature can help. If you are able to be facing a window while you are speaking, or at least have a window to your side (but not on camera), the natural sunlight will provide nice lighting, even if it is not a sunny day. This would mean setting the camera up near the window, but pointing inward, while you face the window area and camera.

Many people choose to setup their video camera against an interior wall. My advice is the opposite, try to set it up against some source of natural light if you can.

If your office is dark, or you are competing with strong light from the rear (often caused by a window or built-in lighting), consider getting a soft light to place in front of your face. It should be a warm hue, so it doesn't create a glare-and-shadow effect, and you want to place it anywhere between the 10 o'clock and 2 o'clock position, assuming 12 o'clock is you looking straight ahead. You can buy built-for-purpose backlights that take up little space online, or you can simply find an old lamp and set it up, if you have the space.

The best light to add to your office is a simple ring light -- the same kind that photographers and YouTubers might use. Most offer a few different types of light (soft, bright white, etc.) as well as the ability to adjust brightness. You can find them on Amazon, you just need a powerful one with plenty of light options, like this one.

Laptop Stand

If your go-to computer for video conferencing is a laptop, consider a laptop stand which can elevate your laptop 3-10 inches off of your desk. It can put the screen at a more natural height relative to your head, and if you choose to use the laptop's built-in camera, avoid you appearing to look down into the computer as if you are staring into a hole.

I have seen people place their laptop on a stack of books in order to make it eye-level. You don't have to do that. Invest a few bucks in a laptop stand, as you will be able to adjust the tilt and other angles.

The best laptop stands are scissors-style, allowing you to easily raise or lower it to your liking. The scissor design allows the stand to fold away easily when not in use.

The Soundance stand is a good, all-purpose one that will not break the bank. (here on Amazon)

External Microphones

I discussed earlier the different ways you might approach the headphones / microphone question. Most people simply use the microphone on their headset, or perhaps on their computer. For some heavy video conference users, or especially those who might be producing recordings or podcasts for future use, a standalone microphone can be a great choice.

The external microphones often resemble the radio microphones of old, with substantial surface area to pick-up the voice intonations and provide ultimate clarity for the person on the other end. They typically require power, which is supplied by a USB connection to a computer.

You can spend a lot of money on a microphone, but unless you are making your living doing podcasts or webinars, you can usually get a good one that will improve your audio quality for less than $100.

If you have the budget for it, I really like the Tula mic. It is portable, has excellent sound quality for those in your meeting, and doing a good job of noise cancellation. (here on Amazon)

Wi-Fi Router

Perhaps one of the most overlooked pieces of equipment is a good wi-fi router. After all, wi-fi is just supposed to work, right? It should not be something you really think about.

Actually, there are a few things you can do to help that wi-fi run on all cylinders. Getting a good router is perhaps the one that is most in your control.

Assuming you have found a quality internet provider, getting a router that can give you a steady signal without slowing it down is critical. Be sure to get a router that can handle at least 1500 Mbps, preferably more.

Router placement is almost as important -- maybe more so -- as the router itself. Put the router in a central place, preferably close to your workspace or office. Placement is probably more important in a large home, because you want to avoid too many walls or other structures that the signal will need to penetrate. Keep in mind that wi-fi signals have a hard time penetrating water, so keep them away from showers and aquariums. It is also best to have your router in a place where it is not stacked on to other electrical equipment, or near a microwave oven or other appliances.

Note that if you are a heavy user of bandwidth and video meetings are critical to your job or your business, consider wiring your computer directly into your network. It might feel old fashioned, but you will greatly diminish the chances of your wi-fi signal having any issues. Anytime you are relying on a signal flowing through the air, interference can happen.

It is all about letting that wi-fi signal fly unfettered to your workspace and devices.

Phone

These days, the phone itself is almost less important than the service it is connected to. A good phone service that provides clear, uninterrupted service can be worth its weight in gold when you are on an important conference call.

Most people choose to use the audio from their computer, laptop, or tablet. As long as your bandwidth can support it and your computer's microphone and speakers are good, this works. Otherwise, don't overlook using your phone for the audio part.

I will share a bit later on the best way to do a video conference with external equipment. But in a pinch, the video from your laptop coupled with the audio from your phone usually gets the job done if your setup isn't conducive to just using your computer.

Regardless of which phone you choose, you will want your phone's mute button to be readily available and easy-to-tap. This is a button you will use often, and you will want to be able to see clearly when you are muted and when you are not. For configurable phones, I often setup one of my side "hotkeys" as an easy-to-locate mute button.

Today's phones are pretty comparable when it comes to voice quality, so we are not wed to any one brand -- iPhone vs. Android vs. other. Perhaps the bigger factor in call quality is that you get a carrier who has excellent coverage in your area. If you plan to do your calls via wi-fi, be sure the bandwidth can handle the typical load so you have clear call quality.

A 10% reduction in call clarity can feel like 50% when you are the person on the other end. Don't skimp, it just isn't worth it.

Tablet or Phone For Video?

A viable option for your video meetings nowadays can be to use the camera on your phone, tablet, or other mobile device. A newer-generation phone or tablet typically has a pretty good camera, capable of giving you the quality of video you will want on a professional meeting. Older phones and tablets, while still OK, are more grainy, have lower resolution and poorer lighting, and some latency. Just be sure you can use the 1080p resolution (available on some newer phones) for video if you want your picture quality to be professional.

Perhaps the biggest consideration to take into account is your bandwidth. You will want to be sure that by adding video bandwidth to your call -- remember it takes about 15x the bandwidth of an audio call -- that you will not compromise both the audio and video portions of your virtual meeting. But if you have the bandwidth and a newer phone (the video on an Iphone 11 is surprisingly good) then you can consider it.

A downside of using this method is that you might end up with two different devices being connected in video-fashion to the meeting. If detailed documents are to be shared during the web meeting, or if you want to be able to easily and clearly see multiple attendees on the screen, a phone or tablet screen might prove a little small. You could well end up logging in using both your phone and computer video, which could get complicated.

A second downside of using a mobile device for a web meeting is that the device might be shaky or unstable during your call -- think of how it looks when you facetime with a friend. That might be alright if you are having a casual chat with a coworker, but if you are trying to impress clients or coworkers from around the globe, it is not ideal.

If you go the mobile device route for your video meeting, you will definitely want a camera stand. The stands I discussed earlier and the ones I recommend work great with phones as well. Check the specs to be sure they would work with your tablet. The other thing you may want to invest in is an app that adds easier-to-use webcam features to your phone. There are many to choose from.

Conferencing Software / Application

There are many conferencing products and applications on the market today. Some are niche providers who do just one things, and others (like Microsoft) integrate their conference call software into other applications.

For most remote workers, your organization or company you are contracting with will provide the conferencing software, so you simply need to get acquainted with that application.

If you are a freelancer or a business owner, you may want to have a go-to application that you use with collaborators and customers. Generally speaking, Zoom, Teams, Slack, Google Meets, and Webex are the ones you will see most.

"It is possible to have too much of a good thing."

—Aesop

Beware Of the Virtual Meeting Traps

The rise of the knowledge worker and the spread of connectivity mean that virtual work will be a bigger part of peoples' careers in the future. On balance, it is a great thing. You can now contribute in a way that you could not before, take a new job without relocating, be productive on a snow day or during an illness outbreak, and contribute less to traffic and congestion.

At the same time, working from home and meeting virtually poses a few challenges. Letting you know about these before they become issues will help you anticipate and plan for them. Here are a few of the tradeoffs of virtual work and what you can do about them.

It can be hard to disconnect or unplug

When you work in an office, you know that the day is done when you leave. When you attend a meeting in-person, the meeting is officially over when the door to the conference room closes behind you. For those who are working virtually, it is a finer line of when you are "on" and when you are not.

Perhaps I oversimplified a bit. After all, there have always been people who take work home with them, and in the day and age of smartphones, many of us are guilty of being online all the time.

There used to be a time when people would stay at the office too late, and enjoy their evenings or weekends, see their families, or engage in hobbies as they wanted too. In most industries, that vice has given way to people being constantly connected. An NIH metastudy on the topic found a number of amusing but also concerning trends with our always-connected existence. There is a wealth of information on the topic, and it begins to diverge from the topic of this book, but it is definitely related. The Society of Human Resource Management (SHRM) has good advice for home-based workers as well: Take breaks throughout the day just as you would at work, and if you feel ill, take a sick day.

My advice, which is not expert advice but rather based on habits of effective people I have witnessed, is to plan your technology into your day, rather than letting it drive you. Begin your day with something other than technology. Put blocks of "work time" into your calendar, to avoid every waking minute being filled with conference calls or discussions. Prioritize the personal things that are important, and unless you are a doctor-on-call or another person critical to get in touch with, detox from your technology during those times.

It can be harder to be fully present at your meetings

In the years of working remotely and handling relatively key meetings virtually, I have witnessed a decreased trend of focus during the meetings -- both from the other attendees, but also from myself. This has the potential to be a scourge, a productivity hit that offsets some of the gains we realize from being able to work more efficiently.

When you are on a conference call, it is easy to multi-task, or even physically be in a place that is not at all conducive to engaging in your meeting. Let's not kid ourselves -- you are not present at your virtual meeting when you are in the checkout line at the market, ordering a coffee, or going through security at the airport. Furthermore, when you have a colleague who forgets to mute their phone, you get a sense of just how much their attention is on anything but the meeting.

Video conferences are decidedly better in terms of people being "present", as you can physically see if people are engaged or not, but there people are still not fully present at all times. Multiple computer screens, pop-ups on your laptop, texting while others are talking, it is easy to see how people are not fully engaged.

Work hard to be in a place where you can fully plug-in to the meeting, and engage with the same concentration and focus that you would if you were sitting in the room with the people. Make sure you examine what is before or after the call on your schedule. If the call ends at 1:59pm and you have a dentist appointment at 2pm, know that you are going to be compromised during the meeting.

Most of all, don't waste peoples' time. If you and some colleagues or clients are trying to hash things out on a call, make the most of it. Engage. Be present. Help the call be productive -- the goal, after all, is to move things forward with the same expectations you would have of any other meeting.

It can be more difficult to form quality relationships

I have been working with one individual for over two years, I will call him Amir. Amir has been my go-to person for a specific task that is critical to my business. We communicate on a near-daily basis during the week. Without Amir, I would have a huge gap in the things I am trying to get done, and my progress would slow considerably.

Amir and I have never met, and I really don't know him.

Part of that is my fault, no doubt. I should set aside time to connect with him more on a personal level, get to know more about his city, his wife and child, and his interests. But he lives in a different part of the world, one that I might not ever get to in my lifetime, and when we are able to talk or email, it is usually about business. I could foresee us continuing to collaborate and partner for 10 years or more, and never meeting or even having a cup of coffee together.

My odd -- but not all that uncommon -- relationship with Amir is representative of so many relationships that are forming in the workplace today. People who rely on each other, work together, are helping each other be successful, but will never actually share one-on-one time together. It happens everywhere. More distributed companies have Executive Assistants supporting Executives in different parts of the country or world, people collaborating on projects from afar, and direct reports who they will hardly ever see.

In a way, it is one of the great things about the world we live in -- talent can contribute to the cause even if it doesn't live in a specific city or region. In another way, though, it takes something away from the culture that makes so many companies great. I surmise that the virtual workplace, and the "free agent" nation where people do not feel loyal to organizations (and organizations do not feel loyal to employees) are related.

Know that if you are a highly-virtual worker, you have to work harder to get to know the person, connect on a different level, and build true trust. Go the extra mile to ask about peoples' weekends when on a phone call, and don't get too far into the relationship without asking more about families, hobbies, interests, and history. If you think about working with someone in a physical office, within the first week you probably know how long their commute is, if they have a family at home, if they are tall, short, fit, not, etc. It is obvious if somebody comes in on Monday morning on a high from the weekend or down in the dumps. You probably even know what kind of coffee drink they prefer from the local shop, and what they like to do for lunch.

All of that good relationship and trust-building gets lost when working virtually, so you have to make an extra effort to cover those bases. Doing so helps build trust, and because trust is so very important to every working relationship and organization, it will be time well spent.

Recap and Checklist:
20 Quick Tips For Effective Virtual Meetings

- ☐ Test your audio and video before joining a meeting to ensure they are working properly.

- ☐ Use a high-quality headset or external microphone for better audio clarity.

- ☐ Make sure you have a stable internet connection to avoid disruptions during the meeting. If you don't have a stable connection, consider augmenting with phone audio.

- ☐ Join the meeting from a well-lit area to ensure good visibility. Front-lighting is best.

- ☐ Position your camera at eye level for a more natural and engaging appearance on video.

- ☐ Use a virtual background if you need to maintain privacy or want to add a professional touch. Otherwise, have a neatly-arranged office setting for a background.

- ☐ Mute yourself when you are not speaking to minimize background noise. Be well-trained on where the mute button is with each app you use.

- ☐ Use keyboard shortcuts to quickly access common features like muting/unmuting, screen sharing, and chat.

- ☐ Familiarize yourself with the platform's settings and customization options to optimize your meeting experience. Customize things like your video background, or how your name and photo show up if you are off-camera.

- ☐ Utilize the screen sharing feature to share documents, presentations, or other content. Know how to share the window, not the entire desktop. 90% of the time, you only want to share a specific window.

- ☐ Use the chat function to communicate with the host or other participants without interrupting the meeting – but don't do it excessively. If you have a key or lengthy point, just speak up.

- ☐ Use the "Raise Hand" feature to indicate that you want to speak or have a question, and encourage others to do the same. When people get comfortable with it, it can streamline interactions.

- ☐ Avoid multitasking during the meeting and give your full attention to the discussion.

- ☐ Beware of outdoor noise that might make its way to your microphone. Things like sirens, birds chirping, or dogs barking could become more of a distraction than you realize.

- ☐ Record the meeting for future reference or for participants who couldn't attend, or for your own replay and improvement if you are trying to get better at presenting.

- ☐ If you plan to use integrated features like the polling or breakout rooms, practice them first so they are second nature.

- ☐ Customize your display name and photo to include your full name and organization for easy identification.

- ☐ Use the "Waiting Room" feature to control who enters the meeting and minimize interruptions.

- ☐ Disable notifications or other distractions on your device to stay focused during the meeting.

- ☐ If you need to join by a combination of phone and computer, merge your identities so you only show up once.

Conclusion

In the end, the move to more tele-work is a great thing. I mentioned the reasons earlier in the book -- you can access talent from anywhere, collaborate more efficiently with people in different cities, commute less, and as we saw with the COVID-19 outbreak, you can keep some level of activity going even when forced to work at home.

The points I raised in the last chapter are more precautionary. Be on the lookout and police yourself so that you don't get too much of a good thing, and that your virtual work can be every bit as engaged and present as your face-to-face work. If you can master it, you will have a competitive advantage and be more successful in the long run.

Since such a huge part of -- and a major area of opportunity for -- virtual work is mastering conference calls and videoconferences, I focused the majority of this book there. Being better at communicating virtually will allow workers to get more done, sales people to advance discussions with more clients, leaders to coach and lead better, and employees to have more success in their careers.

Most of all, I think that if we are able to use these communication channels effectively, we can unleash the potential of remote work in a way that we have not been able to before. We will allow more people to work from home, more people to live as digital nomads, and -- perhaps most importantly -- we will be able to collaborate with people regardless of where they live, opening up new frontiers enabled by today's technology.

A Very Important Request

I hope you learned something from this book. As much as I love to get letters and notes from my readers -- I treasure them all -- the best way you can help me is to leave a review on Amazon. I will see it, and it will help allow others to determine if this book is right for them.

You can leave that review here on Amazon, where you found this book.

Finally, if you enjoyed this book, I would be thrilled if you would check out my other book. It is a practical, hands-on guide to career management for the professional. It was a labor of love, and provides advice that I think is timeless and applies to any career. You can find it here.

Thank you!

www.ingramcontent.com/pod-product-compliance
Lightning Source LLC
Chambersburg PA
CBHW030950240526
45463CB00016B/2331